50 Family Favorites Recipes for Home

By: Kelly Johnson

Table of Contents

- Spaghetti and Meatballs
- Chicken Alfredo
- Beef Tacos
- Baked Ziti
- Chicken Parmesan
- Vegetable Stir-Fry
- Meatloaf
- Chili
- Shepherd's Pie
- Homemade Pizza
- BBQ Ribs
- Chicken Noodle Soup
- Sloppy Joes
- Fish Tacos
- Macaroni and Cheese
- Pancakes
- Waffles
- Stuffed Bell Peppers
- Grilled Cheese Sandwiches
- Caesar Salad
- Beef Stroganoff
- Roasted Chicken
- Lasagna
- Sweet and Sour Pork
- Chicken Quesadillas
- Corn Chowder
- Egg Fried Rice
- Shrimp Scampi
- Broccoli Cheddar Soup
- Pot Roast
- Fettuccine Alfredo
- Tater Tot Casserole
- Stuffed Shells
- Chicken Fajitas
- Quiche

- Clam Chowder
- Beef Enchiladas
- Teriyaki Chicken
- Cabbage Rolls
- Thai Peanut Noodles
- Chicken and Rice Casserole
- Pumpkin Bread
- Banana Bread
- Chocolate Chip Cookies
- Brownies
- Apple Crisp
- Fruit Salad
- Cinnamon Rolls
- Rice Pudding
- Lemon Bars

Spaghetti and Meatballs

Ingredients:

- **For the Meatballs:**
    - 1 lb ground beef
    - 1/2 cup breadcrumbs
    - 1/4 cup grated Parmesan cheese
    - 1 egg
    - 2 cloves garlic, minced
    - 1 tsp Italian seasoning
    - Salt and pepper to taste
- **For the Sauce:**
    - 1 can (28 oz) crushed tomatoes
    - 1 onion, chopped
    - 2 cloves garlic, minced
    - 1 tsp sugar
    - Olive oil for sautéing
    - Salt and pepper to taste
- **For the Pasta:**
    - 8 oz spaghetti

Instructions:

1. **Preheat Oven:** Preheat oven to 400°F (200°C).
2. **Make Meatballs:** In a bowl, combine ground beef, breadcrumbs, Parmesan, egg, garlic, Italian seasoning, salt, and pepper. Form into meatballs.
3. **Bake Meatballs:** Place meatballs on a baking sheet and bake for 20 minutes.
4. **Make Sauce:** In a pot, heat olive oil over medium heat. Sauté onion and garlic until softened. Add crushed tomatoes, sugar, salt, and pepper. Simmer for 15 minutes.
5. **Cook Pasta:** Cook spaghetti according to package instructions.
6. **Combine:** Add baked meatballs to the sauce. Serve over spaghetti.

Chicken Alfredo

Ingredients:

- 8 oz fettuccine
- 1 lb chicken breast, sliced
- 1 cup heavy cream
- 1 cup grated Parmesan cheese
- 2 tbsp butter
- 2 cloves garlic, minced
- Salt and pepper to taste
- Fresh parsley for garnish

Instructions:

1. **Cook Pasta:** Cook fettuccine according to package instructions; drain.
2. **Cook Chicken:** In a skillet, melt butter over medium heat. Add chicken, garlic, salt, and pepper; cook until chicken is cooked through.
3. **Make Sauce:** Stir in heavy cream and bring to a simmer. Add Parmesan cheese and stir until melted and smooth.
4. **Combine:** Toss cooked fettuccine with the sauce and chicken.
5. **Serve:** Garnish with fresh parsley and extra Parmesan if desired.

Beef Tacos

Ingredients:

- 1 lb ground beef
- 1 packet taco seasoning
- 8 taco shells
- Toppings: shredded lettuce, diced tomatoes, cheese, sour cream, salsa

Instructions:

1. **Cook Beef:** In a skillet, cook ground beef over medium heat until browned. Drain excess fat.
2. **Add Seasoning:** Stir in taco seasoning with the recommended amount of water. Simmer for 5 minutes.
3. **Assemble Tacos:** Fill taco shells with seasoned beef and desired toppings.

Baked Ziti

Ingredients:

- 12 oz ziti pasta
- 1 lb ground beef or Italian sausage
- 1 jar (24 oz) marinara sauce
- 2 cups ricotta cheese
- 2 cups shredded mozzarella cheese
- 1/2 cup grated Parmesan cheese
- 1 tsp Italian seasoning

Instructions:

1. **Preheat Oven:** Preheat oven to 375°F (190°C).
2. **Cook Pasta:** Cook ziti according to package instructions; drain.
3. **Cook Meat:** In a skillet, brown ground beef or sausage. Drain excess fat and stir in marinara sauce.
4. **Combine:** In a large bowl, mix cooked ziti, meat sauce, ricotta, Italian seasoning, and half of the mozzarella.
5. **Bake:** Pour into a baking dish, top with remaining mozzarella and Parmesan. Bake for 25-30 minutes until bubbly.

Chicken Parmesan

Ingredients:

- 2 chicken breasts, flattened
- 1 cup breadcrumbs
- 1/2 cup grated Parmesan cheese
- 1 egg, beaten
- 1 cup marinara sauce
- 1 cup shredded mozzarella cheese
- Olive oil for frying

Instructions:

1. **Preheat Oven:** Preheat oven to 375°F (190°C).
2. **Bread Chicken:** Dip chicken breasts in beaten egg, then coat with a mixture of breadcrumbs and Parmesan.
3. **Fry Chicken:** In a skillet, heat olive oil over medium heat. Fry chicken until golden brown on both sides.
4. **Bake:** Place fried chicken in a baking dish, top with marinara and mozzarella. Bake for 20 minutes until cheese is melted.

Vegetable Stir-Fry

Ingredients:

- 2 cups mixed vegetables (broccoli, bell peppers, carrots)
- 2 cloves garlic, minced
- 1 tbsp ginger, minced
- 3 tbsp soy sauce
- 2 tbsp vegetable oil
- Cooked rice for serving

Instructions:

1. **Heat Oil:** In a large skillet or wok, heat vegetable oil over high heat.
2. **Stir-Fry Veggies:** Add garlic and ginger; sauté for 30 seconds. Add mixed vegetables and stir-fry until tender-crisp.
3. **Add Sauce:** Stir in soy sauce and cook for another minute.
4. **Serve:** Serve over cooked rice.

Meatloaf

Ingredients:

- 1 lb ground beef
- 1 cup breadcrumbs
- 1/2 cup milk
- 1 egg
- 1 onion, chopped
- 1/4 cup ketchup
- 1 tsp Worcestershire sauce
- Salt and pepper to taste

Instructions:

1. **Preheat Oven:** Preheat oven to 350°F (175°C).
2. **Mix Ingredients:** In a bowl, combine all ingredients and mix well.
3. **Shape Loaf:** Form mixture into a loaf shape and place in a baking dish.
4. **Bake:** Bake for 1 hour, or until cooked through. Serve with extra ketchup if desired.

Chili

Ingredients:

- 1 lb ground beef
- 1 can (15 oz) kidney beans, drained
- 1 can (15 oz) diced tomatoes
- 1 onion, chopped
- 2 cloves garlic, minced
- 2 tbsp chili powder
- 1 tsp cumin
- Salt and pepper to taste

Instructions:

1. **Cook Beef:** In a large pot, cook ground beef with onion and garlic until browned; drain excess fat.
2. **Add Ingredients:** Stir in kidney beans, diced tomatoes, chili powder, cumin, salt, and pepper.
3. **Simmer:** Simmer for 20-30 minutes, stirring occasionally.
4. **Serve:** Serve hot, with toppings like cheese or sour cream if desired.

Shepherd's Pie

Ingredients:

- 1 lb ground beef or lamb
- 1 onion, chopped
- 2 carrots, diced
- 2 cups frozen peas
- 2 tbsp tomato paste
- 1 cup beef broth
- 4 cups mashed potatoes
- Salt and pepper to taste

Instructions:

1. **Preheat Oven:** Preheat oven to 400°F (200°C).
2. **Cook Meat:** In a skillet, cook ground meat with onion and carrots until browned; drain excess fat. Stir in tomato paste, peas, beef broth, salt, and pepper.
3. **Assemble:** Transfer meat mixture to a baking dish and spread mashed potatoes on top.
4. **Bake:** Bake for 25-30 minutes until golden on top.

Enjoy these comforting and delicious dishes!

Homemade Pizza

Ingredients:

- **For the Dough:**
    - 2 cups all-purpose flour
    - 1 packet (2 1/4 tsp) instant yeast
    - 1 tsp salt
    - 1 tsp sugar
    - 3/4 cup warm water
    - 1 tbsp olive oil
- **For the Toppings:**
    - 1 cup pizza sauce
    - 2 cups shredded mozzarella cheese
    - Your choice of toppings (pepperoni, bell peppers, mushrooms, olives, etc.)

Instructions:

1. **Make Dough:** In a bowl, combine flour, yeast, salt, and sugar. Add warm water and olive oil. Mix until a dough forms, then knead for about 5 minutes until smooth.
2. **Let Rise:** Place in an oiled bowl, cover, and let rise for 1 hour.
3. **Preheat Oven:** Preheat oven to 475°F (245°C).
4. **Shape Pizza:** Roll out the dough on a floured surface to your desired thickness. Transfer to a pizza stone or baking sheet.
5. **Add Toppings:** Spread pizza sauce on the dough, sprinkle with cheese, and add your toppings.
6. **Bake:** Bake for 12-15 minutes until the crust is golden and cheese is bubbly.

BBQ Ribs

Ingredients:

- 2 lbs pork ribs
- 1 cup BBQ sauce
- 1 tbsp brown sugar
- 1 tsp paprika
- 1 tsp garlic powder
- 1 tsp onion powder
- Salt and pepper to taste

Instructions:

1. **Preheat Oven:** Preheat oven to 300°F (150°C).
2. **Prepare Ribs:** Season ribs with brown sugar, paprika, garlic powder, onion powder, salt, and pepper.
3. **Wrap and Bake:** Wrap ribs in foil and place on a baking sheet. Bake for 2.5 to 3 hours until tender.
4. **Add BBQ Sauce:** Unwrap ribs, brush with BBQ sauce, and broil for 5-10 minutes until caramelized.

Chicken Noodle Soup

Ingredients:

- 1 lb chicken breast, diced
- 4 cups chicken broth
- 2 cups egg noodles
- 2 carrots, sliced
- 2 celery stalks, sliced
- 1 onion, chopped
- 2 cloves garlic, minced
- Salt and pepper to taste
- Fresh parsley for garnish

Instructions:

1. **Cook Chicken:** In a large pot, combine chicken and broth. Bring to a boil, then simmer until chicken is cooked through; remove and shred.
2. **Sauté Veggies:** In the same pot, add onion, carrots, celery, and garlic; sauté until softened.
3. **Add Noodles:** Stir in egg noodles and cook until tender.
4. **Combine:** Return shredded chicken to the pot, season with salt and pepper, and simmer for a few more minutes.
5. **Serve:** Garnish with fresh parsley before serving.

Sloppy Joes

Ingredients:

- 1 lb ground beef
- 1 onion, chopped
- 1/2 cup ketchup
- 1 tbsp mustard
- 1 tbsp brown sugar
- 1 tbsp Worcestershire sauce
- Salt and pepper to taste
- Burger buns for serving

Instructions:

1. **Cook Beef:** In a skillet, cook ground beef and onion over medium heat until browned; drain excess fat.
2. **Add Sauce:** Stir in ketchup, mustard, brown sugar, Worcestershire sauce, salt, and pepper. Simmer for 10 minutes.
3. **Serve:** Spoon mixture onto burger buns and serve hot.

Fish Tacos

Ingredients:

- 1 lb white fish (like tilapia or cod)
- 1 tsp cumin
- 1 tsp paprika
- Salt and pepper to taste
- 8 corn tortillas
- Toppings: shredded cabbage, diced tomatoes, avocado, lime wedges

Instructions:

1. **Season Fish:** Season fish with cumin, paprika, salt, and pepper.
2. **Cook Fish:** Grill or pan-fry fish for 3-4 minutes per side until cooked through.
3. **Warm Tortillas:** Warm tortillas in a skillet or microwave.
4. **Assemble Tacos:** Flake fish into pieces and fill tortillas. Top with cabbage, tomatoes, avocado, and a squeeze of lime.

Macaroni and Cheese

Ingredients:

- 8 oz elbow macaroni
- 2 cups shredded cheese (cheddar and/or mozzarella)
- 2 cups milk
- 1/4 cup butter
- 1/4 cup flour
- 1/2 tsp mustard powder
- Salt and pepper to taste

Instructions:

1. **Cook Pasta:** Cook macaroni according to package instructions; drain and set aside.
2. **Make Cheese Sauce:** In a saucepan, melt butter over medium heat. Whisk in flour and cook for 1-2 minutes. Gradually whisk in milk, stirring until thickened.
3. **Add Cheese:** Stir in shredded cheese, mustard powder, salt, and pepper until melted and smooth.
4. **Combine:** Fold in cooked macaroni. Serve warm.

Pancakes

Ingredients:

- 1 cup all-purpose flour
- 2 tbsp sugar
- 2 tsp baking powder
- 1/2 tsp salt
- 1 cup milk
- 1 egg
- 2 tbsp melted butter

Instructions:

1. **Mix Dry Ingredients:** In a bowl, whisk together flour, sugar, baking powder, and salt.
2. **Mix Wet Ingredients:** In another bowl, combine milk, egg, and melted butter.
3. **Combine Mixtures:** Pour wet ingredients into dry and mix until just combined.
4. **Cook Pancakes:** Heat a skillet over medium heat. Pour batter onto the skillet and cook until bubbles form; flip and cook until golden.

Waffles

Ingredients:

- 2 cups all-purpose flour
- 2 tbsp sugar
- 1 tbsp baking powder
- 1/2 tsp salt
- 2 eggs
- 1 3/4 cups milk
- 1/2 cup vegetable oil

Instructions:

1. **Mix Dry Ingredients:** In a large bowl, whisk together flour, sugar, baking powder, and salt.
2. **Mix Wet Ingredients:** In another bowl, combine eggs, milk, and vegetable oil.
3. **Combine Mixtures:** Pour wet ingredients into dry and stir until just mixed.
4. **Cook Waffles:** Preheat waffle maker and pour batter according to the manufacturer's instructions. Cook until golden brown.

Stuffed Bell Peppers

Ingredients:

- 4 bell peppers (any color)
- 1 lb ground beef or turkey
- 1 cup cooked rice
- 1 can (15 oz) diced tomatoes
- 1 cup shredded cheese
- 1 tsp Italian seasoning
- Salt and pepper to taste

Instructions:

1. **Preheat Oven:** Preheat oven to 375°F (190°C).
2. **Prepare Peppers:** Cut tops off bell peppers and remove seeds.
3. **Make Filling:** In a skillet, cook ground meat until browned. Stir in cooked rice, diced tomatoes, Italian seasoning, salt, and pepper.
4. **Stuff Peppers:** Fill each bell pepper with the meat mixture and place in a baking dish.
5. **Bake:** Top with cheese and bake for 25-30 minutes until peppers are tender.

Enjoy these hearty and delicious recipes!

Grilled Cheese Sandwiches

Ingredients:

- 4 slices of bread (your choice)
- 4 slices of cheese (cheddar, American, or your favorite)
- 2 tbsp butter

Instructions:

1. **Preheat Skillet:** Heat a skillet over medium heat.
2. **Butter Bread:** Spread butter on one side of each slice of bread.
3. **Assemble Sandwich:** Place one slice of bread, butter side down, in the skillet. Top with cheese and another slice of bread, butter side up.
4. **Cook:** Grill until golden brown on one side, then flip and cook until the cheese is melted and the other side is golden brown.
5. **Serve:** Slice and enjoy warm.

Caesar Salad

Ingredients:

- 1 head romaine lettuce, chopped
- 1/2 cup Caesar dressing
- 1/4 cup grated Parmesan cheese
- Croutons
- Freshly ground black pepper

Instructions:

1. **Combine Ingredients:** In a large bowl, combine chopped romaine lettuce, Caesar dressing, and grated Parmesan.
2. **Add Croutons:** Toss in croutons and sprinkle with black pepper.
3. **Serve:** Serve immediately as a side salad.

Beef Stroganoff

Ingredients:

- 1 lb beef sirloin, sliced into strips
- 1 onion, chopped
- 2 cloves garlic, minced
- 8 oz mushrooms, sliced
- 2 cups beef broth
- 1 cup sour cream
- 2 tbsp flour
- 1 tbsp Worcestershire sauce
- Salt and pepper to taste
- Cooked egg noodles for serving

Instructions:

1. **Brown Beef:** In a skillet, cook beef strips over medium-high heat until browned. Remove and set aside.
2. **Sauté Veggies:** In the same skillet, add onion, garlic, and mushrooms; sauté until softened.
3. **Make Sauce:** Stir in flour, then add beef broth and Worcestershire sauce. Simmer for 5-7 minutes.
4. **Add Beef and Sour Cream:** Return beef to the skillet, stir in sour cream, and season with salt and pepper.
5. **Serve:** Serve over cooked egg noodles.

Roasted Chicken

Ingredients:

- 1 whole chicken (about 4-5 lbs)
- 2 tbsp olive oil
- 1 lemon, halved
- 4 cloves garlic, smashed
- Fresh herbs (rosemary, thyme, or parsley)
- Salt and pepper to taste

Instructions:

1. **Preheat Oven:** Preheat oven to 425°F (220°C).
2. **Prepare Chicken:** Pat chicken dry, then rub with olive oil, salt, and pepper. Stuff cavity with lemon halves, garlic, and herbs.
3. **Roast Chicken:** Place chicken in a roasting pan and roast for about 1.5 hours, or until the internal temperature reaches 165°F (75°C).
4. **Rest and Serve:** Let rest for 10-15 minutes before carving.

Lasagna

Ingredients:

- 9 lasagna noodles
- 1 lb ground beef or sausage
- 2 cups ricotta cheese
- 2 cups shredded mozzarella cheese
- 1/2 cup grated Parmesan cheese
- 2 cups marinara sauce
- 1 egg
- 1 tsp Italian seasoning
- Salt and pepper to taste

Instructions:

1. **Preheat Oven:** Preheat oven to 375°F (190°C).
2. **Cook Noodles:** Cook lasagna noodles according to package instructions; drain.
3. **Cook Meat:** In a skillet, brown ground meat; drain excess fat. Stir in marinara sauce.
4. **Mix Cheese:** In a bowl, combine ricotta cheese, egg, Italian seasoning, salt, and pepper.
5. **Assemble Lasagna:** In a baking dish, layer noodles, meat sauce, ricotta mixture, and mozzarella. Repeat layers, finishing with mozzarella and Parmesan on top.
6. **Bake:** Cover with foil and bake for 25 minutes, then uncover and bake for an additional 15 minutes until bubbly.

Sweet and Sour Pork

Ingredients:

- 1 lb pork tenderloin, cubed
- 1 bell pepper, chopped
- 1 onion, chopped
- 1 can (20 oz) pineapple chunks, drained
- 1/2 cup sweet and sour sauce
- 2 tbsp soy sauce
- 1 tbsp vegetable oil

Instructions:

1. **Cook Pork:** In a skillet, heat vegetable oil over medium heat. Add pork and cook until browned.
2. **Add Vegetables:** Stir in bell pepper, onion, and pineapple; cook until vegetables are tender.
3. **Add Sauce:** Stir in sweet and sour sauce and soy sauce; simmer for 5 minutes.
4. **Serve:** Serve over rice or noodles.

Chicken Quesadillas

Ingredients:

- 2 cups cooked chicken, shredded
- 1 cup shredded cheese (cheddar or Monterey Jack)
- 4 flour tortillas
- 1/2 cup salsa
- 1 tbsp vegetable oil

Instructions:

1. **Heat Skillet:** In a skillet, heat vegetable oil over medium heat.
2. **Assemble Quesadillas:** Place one tortilla in the skillet, sprinkle half with cheese, add chicken, salsa, and top with more cheese. Fold tortilla in half.
3. **Cook Quesadilla:** Cook until cheese melts and tortilla is golden, about 3-4 minutes per side.
4. **Slice and Serve:** Cut into wedges and serve with sour cream or guacamole.

Corn Chowder

Ingredients:

- 4 cups corn (fresh, frozen, or canned)
- 1 onion, chopped
- 2 potatoes, diced
- 4 cups chicken broth
- 1 cup heavy cream
- 2 tbsp butter
- Salt and pepper to taste

Instructions:

1. **Sauté Onion:** In a large pot, melt butter over medium heat. Add onion and cook until softened.
2. **Add Potatoes and Corn:** Stir in diced potatoes, corn, and chicken broth. Bring to a boil, then simmer until potatoes are tender, about 15-20 minutes.
3. **Blend (optional):** For a creamier texture, blend part of the chowder with an immersion blender.
4. **Add Cream:** Stir in heavy cream, season with salt and pepper, and heat through. Serve warm.

Enjoy these delicious and comforting recipes!

Egg Fried Rice

Ingredients:

- 3 cups cooked rice (preferably day-old)
- 2 eggs, beaten
- 1 cup mixed vegetables (peas, carrots, corn)
- 2 green onions, sliced
- 3 tbsp soy sauce
- 2 tbsp vegetable oil
- Salt and pepper to taste

Instructions:

1. **Heat Oil:** In a large skillet or wok, heat vegetable oil over medium-high heat.
2. **Scramble Eggs:** Add beaten eggs and scramble until fully cooked. Remove and set aside.
3. **Cook Vegetables:** In the same skillet, add mixed vegetables and cook until tender.
4. **Add Rice:** Stir in the cooked rice, soy sauce, and scrambled eggs. Mix well and season with salt and pepper.
5. **Garnish:** Sprinkle with green onions before serving.

Shrimp Scampi

Ingredients:

- 1 lb shrimp, peeled and deveined
- 4 cloves garlic, minced
- 1/4 cup butter
- 1/4 cup olive oil
- 1/4 cup white wine (optional)
- Juice of 1 lemon
- Salt and pepper to taste
- Fresh parsley, chopped
- Cooked pasta (linguine or spaghetti) for serving

Instructions:

1. **Cook Shrimp:** In a large skillet, melt butter and olive oil over medium heat. Add garlic and sauté until fragrant.
2. **Add Shrimp:** Add shrimp, season with salt and pepper, and cook until pink (about 3-4 minutes).
3. **Add Wine and Lemon:** Stir in white wine (if using) and lemon juice, cooking for an additional 2 minutes.
4. **Serve:** Toss with cooked pasta and garnish with fresh parsley.

Broccoli Cheddar Soup

Ingredients:

- 4 cups broccoli florets
- 1 onion, chopped
- 2 carrots, diced
- 3 cups vegetable or chicken broth
- 1 cup heavy cream
- 2 cups shredded cheddar cheese
- 3 tbsp butter
- 1/4 cup flour
- Salt and pepper to taste

Instructions:

1. **Sauté Vegetables:** In a large pot, melt butter over medium heat. Add onion and carrots; cook until softened.
2. **Add Broccoli and Broth:** Stir in broccoli and broth; bring to a boil. Reduce heat and simmer until broccoli is tender.
3. **Thicken Soup:** In a separate bowl, whisk together flour and cream. Slowly stir into the pot and simmer until thickened.
4. **Add Cheese:** Stir in cheddar cheese until melted. Season with salt and pepper. Serve warm.

Pot Roast

Ingredients:

- 3-4 lbs beef chuck roast
- 4 cups beef broth
- 4 carrots, chopped
- 4 potatoes, quartered
- 1 onion, quartered
- 3 cloves garlic, minced
- 2 tbsp olive oil
- 1 tbsp Worcestershire sauce
- Salt and pepper to taste

Instructions:

1. **Brown Roast:** In a large pot or slow cooker, heat olive oil over medium-high heat. Season the roast with salt and pepper, then brown on all sides.
2. **Add Ingredients:** Add broth, carrots, potatoes, onion, garlic, and Worcestershire sauce.
3. **Cook:** Cover and cook on low for 6-8 hours in a slow cooker, or in the oven at 325°F (160°C) for 3-4 hours until tender.
4. **Serve:** Slice and serve with the vegetables and broth.

Fettuccine Alfredo

Ingredients:

- 8 oz fettuccine
- 1/2 cup butter
- 1 cup heavy cream
- 1 1/2 cups grated Parmesan cheese
- 2 cloves garlic, minced
- Salt and pepper to taste
- Fresh parsley, chopped (for garnish)

Instructions:

1. **Cook Pasta:** Cook fettuccine according to package instructions; drain.
2. **Make Sauce:** In a large skillet, melt butter over medium heat. Add garlic and cook until fragrant.
3. **Add Cream:** Stir in heavy cream and simmer for 2-3 minutes.
4. **Add Cheese:** Gradually whisk in Parmesan cheese until melted and smooth.
5. **Combine:** Toss cooked fettuccine in the sauce, season with salt and pepper, and garnish with parsley before serving.

Tater Tot Casserole

Ingredients:

- 1 lb ground beef
- 1 can (10.5 oz) cream of mushroom soup
- 1 cup frozen mixed vegetables
- 2 cups shredded cheese (cheddar or your choice)
- 1 bag (32 oz) tater tots
- Salt and pepper to taste

Instructions:

1. **Preheat Oven:** Preheat oven to 350°F (175°C).
2. **Cook Beef:** In a skillet, cook ground beef over medium heat until browned; drain excess fat.
3. **Combine Ingredients:** In a large bowl, mix cooked beef, cream of mushroom soup, mixed vegetables, and half of the cheese.
4. **Assemble Casserole:** Pour the mixture into a baking dish and top with tater tots.
5. **Bake:** Bake for 25-30 minutes. Sprinkle with remaining cheese and bake for an additional 5-10 minutes until golden.

Stuffed Shells

Ingredients:

- 12 jumbo pasta shells
- 1 1/2 cups ricotta cheese
- 1 cup shredded mozzarella cheese
- 1/2 cup grated Parmesan cheese
- 2 cups marinara sauce
- 1 egg
- 1 tsp Italian seasoning
- Salt and pepper to taste

Instructions:

1. **Preheat Oven:** Preheat oven to 375°F (190°C).
2. **Cook Shells:** Cook pasta shells according to package instructions; drain and let cool.
3. **Mix Filling:** In a bowl, combine ricotta, mozzarella, Parmesan, egg, Italian seasoning, salt, and pepper.
4. **Stuff Shells:** Fill each shell with the cheese mixture and place in a baking dish.
5. **Add Sauce:** Pour marinara sauce over the stuffed shells and sprinkle with extra mozzarella.
6. **Bake:** Cover with foil and bake for 25 minutes. Remove foil and bake for an additional 10 minutes until cheese is bubbly.

Chicken Fajitas

Ingredients:

- 1 lb chicken breast, sliced
- 1 bell pepper, sliced
- 1 onion, sliced
- 2 tbsp olive oil
- 2 tsp fajita seasoning
- Tortillas for serving
- Toppings: sour cream, salsa, avocado

Instructions:

1. **Cook Chicken:** In a skillet, heat olive oil over medium heat. Add chicken and cook until browned.
2. **Add Vegetables:** Stir in bell pepper, onion, and fajita seasoning; cook until vegetables are tender.
3. **Serve:** Serve with warm tortillas and your choice of toppings.

Enjoy these delicious and hearty recipes!

Quiche

Ingredients:

- 1 pre-made pie crust
- 4 large eggs
- 1 cup heavy cream or milk
- 1 cup shredded cheese (cheddar, Swiss, or your choice)
- 1 cup vegetables (spinach, mushrooms, bell peppers, etc.)
- 1/2 cup cooked meat (ham, bacon, or sausage, optional)
- Salt and pepper to taste

Instructions:

1. **Preheat Oven:** Preheat oven to 375°F (190°C).
2. **Prepare Filling:** In a bowl, whisk together eggs, cream, salt, and pepper. Stir in cheese, vegetables, and meat if using.
3. **Fill Pie Crust:** Pour the mixture into the pie crust.
4. **Bake:** Bake for 35-40 minutes until the center is set and the top is golden. Let cool slightly before slicing.

Clam Chowder

Ingredients:

- 4 slices bacon, chopped
- 1 onion, chopped
- 2 celery stalks, chopped
- 2 cups potatoes, diced
- 2 cans (6.5 oz each) chopped clams (with juice)
- 2 cups chicken broth
- 1 cup heavy cream
- Salt and pepper to taste
- Fresh parsley for garnish

Instructions:

1. **Cook Bacon:** In a large pot, cook bacon over medium heat until crispy. Remove and set aside, leaving drippings in the pot.
2. **Sauté Veggies:** Add onion and celery to the pot; cook until softened.
3. **Add Potatoes and Broth:** Stir in potatoes, clams (with juice), and chicken broth. Bring to a boil, then simmer until potatoes are tender (about 15 minutes).
4. **Add Cream:** Stir in heavy cream and season with salt and pepper. Heat through and garnish with parsley before serving.

Beef Enchiladas

Ingredients:

- 1 lb ground beef
- 1 cup onion, chopped
- 2 cups enchilada sauce (store-bought or homemade)
- 1 cup shredded cheese (cheddar or Monterey Jack)
- 8 flour tortillas
- 1 can (15 oz) black beans (optional)
- Salt and pepper to taste

Instructions:

1. **Preheat Oven:** Preheat oven to 350°F (175°C).
2. **Cook Beef:** In a skillet, brown ground beef and onion over medium heat; drain excess fat. Season with salt and pepper.
3. **Fill Tortillas:** Mix 1 cup of enchilada sauce with the beef mixture. Fill each tortilla with the mixture and roll up.
4. **Assemble Dish:** Place enchiladas seam-side down in a baking dish. Pour remaining enchilada sauce over the top and sprinkle with cheese.
5. **Bake:** Bake for 20-25 minutes until cheese is melted and bubbly.

Teriyaki Chicken

Ingredients:

- 1 lb chicken thighs or breasts, cut into bite-sized pieces
- 1/2 cup teriyaki sauce
- 1 tbsp vegetable oil
- 1 cup broccoli florets
- 1 bell pepper, sliced
- Sesame seeds for garnish
- Cooked rice for serving

Instructions:

1. **Cook Chicken:** In a skillet, heat oil over medium-high heat. Add chicken and cook until browned and cooked through.
2. **Add Vegetables:** Stir in broccoli and bell pepper; cook until tender.
3. **Add Sauce:** Pour teriyaki sauce over the chicken and vegetables; cook for an additional 2-3 minutes to heat through.
4. **Serve:** Serve over cooked rice and garnish with sesame seeds.

Cabbage Rolls

Ingredients:

- 1 head cabbage
- 1 lb ground beef or turkey
- 1 cup cooked rice
- 1 can (15 oz) tomato sauce
- 1/2 cup onion, chopped
- 1 tsp garlic powder
- Salt and pepper to taste
- 1 can (15 oz) diced tomatoes (for topping)

Instructions:

1. **Prepare Cabbage:** Bring a large pot of water to a boil. Carefully remove cabbage leaves and blanch for 2-3 minutes until pliable.
2. **Make Filling:** In a bowl, combine ground meat, cooked rice, onion, garlic powder, salt, and pepper.
3. **Fill Rolls:** Place a portion of the filling in the center of each cabbage leaf and roll up tightly, tucking in the sides.
4. **Assemble:** Place cabbage rolls seam-side down in a baking dish. Pour tomato sauce and diced tomatoes over the top.
5. **Bake:** Cover and bake at 350°F (175°C) for about 1 hour, until cooked through.

Thai Peanut Noodles

Ingredients:

- 8 oz rice noodles or spaghetti
- 1/2 cup peanut butter
- 1/4 cup soy sauce
- 2 tbsp honey or brown sugar
- 2 tbsp rice vinegar
- 1 tbsp sesame oil
- 2 cups mixed vegetables (bell peppers, carrots, broccoli)
- Chopped peanuts and cilantro for garnish

Instructions:

1. **Cook Noodles:** Cook noodles according to package instructions; drain and set aside.
2. **Make Sauce:** In a bowl, whisk together peanut butter, soy sauce, honey, rice vinegar, and sesame oil until smooth.
3. **Stir-Fry Vegetables:** In a skillet, stir-fry mixed vegetables until tender.
4. **Combine:** Add cooked noodles and peanut sauce to the skillet; toss to combine and heat through.
5. **Serve:** Garnish with chopped peanuts and cilantro before serving.

Chicken and Rice Casserole

Ingredients:

- 2 cups cooked chicken, shredded
- 1 cup rice (uncooked)
- 2 cups chicken broth
- 1 cup frozen mixed vegetables
- 1 can (10.5 oz) cream of chicken soup
- 1 tsp garlic powder
- Salt and pepper to taste

Instructions:

1. **Preheat Oven:** Preheat oven to 375°F (190°C).
2. **Combine Ingredients:** In a large bowl, mix shredded chicken, uncooked rice, chicken broth, mixed vegetables, cream of chicken soup, garlic powder, salt, and pepper.
3. **Transfer to Baking Dish:** Pour mixture into a greased baking dish.
4. **Bake:** Cover with foil and bake for 45-55 minutes until rice is tender. Remove foil and bake for an additional 10 minutes.

Pumpkin Bread

Ingredients:

- 1 cup canned pumpkin puree
- 1/2 cup vegetable oil
- 1 cup sugar
- 2 large eggs
- 1 1/2 cups all-purpose flour
- 1 tsp baking soda
- 1/2 tsp baking powder
- 1 tsp cinnamon
- 1/2 tsp nutmeg
- 1/2 tsp salt

Instructions:

1. **Preheat Oven:** Preheat oven to 350°F (175°C). Grease a loaf pan.
2. **Mix Wet Ingredients:** In a large bowl, mix pumpkin, oil, sugar, and eggs until smooth.
3. **Combine Dry Ingredients:** In another bowl, whisk together flour, baking soda, baking powder, cinnamon, nutmeg, and salt.
4. **Combine Mixtures:** Gradually add dry ingredients to the pumpkin mixture, stirring until just combined.
5. **Bake:** Pour batter into the prepared loaf pan and bake for 60-70 minutes, or until a toothpick comes out clean. Let cool before slicing.

Enjoy these hearty and delicious recipes!

Banana Bread

Ingredients:

- 3 ripe bananas, mashed
- 1/3 cup melted butter
- 1 cup sugar
- 1 egg, beaten
- 1 tsp vanilla extract
- 1 tsp baking soda
- Pinch of salt
- 1 1/2 cups all-purpose flour

Instructions:

1. **Preheat Oven:** Preheat oven to 350°F (175°C). Grease a 4x8 inch loaf pan.
2. **Mix Wet Ingredients:** In a mixing bowl, mix melted butter into the mashed bananas.
3. **Add Remaining Ingredients:** Stir in sugar, beaten egg, and vanilla. Sprinkle the baking soda and salt over the mixture, then mix in the flour.
4. **Bake:** Pour batter into the prepared pan and bake for 60-65 minutes. Cool in the pan for a few minutes before transferring to a wire rack.

Chocolate Chip Cookies

Ingredients:

- 1 cup butter, softened
- 3/4 cup sugar
- 3/4 cup brown sugar, packed
- 1 tsp vanilla extract
- 2 large eggs
- 2 1/4 cups all-purpose flour
- 1 tsp baking soda
- 1/2 tsp salt
- 2 cups chocolate chips

Instructions:

1. **Preheat Oven:** Preheat oven to 375°F (190°C).
2. **Mix Wet Ingredients:** In a large bowl, cream together butter, sugar, brown sugar, and vanilla. Beat in eggs one at a time.
3. **Add Dry Ingredients:** Combine flour, baking soda, and salt; gradually add to the creamed mixture. Stir in chocolate chips.
4. **Bake:** Drop by rounded tablespoon onto ungreased baking sheets. Bake for 9-11 minutes until golden.

Brownies

Ingredients:

- 1/2 cup butter
- 1 cup sugar
- 2 large eggs
- 1 tsp vanilla extract
- 1/3 cup cocoa powder
- 1/2 cup all-purpose flour
- 1/4 tsp salt
- 1/4 tsp baking powder

Instructions:

1. **Preheat Oven:** Preheat oven to 350°F (175°C). Grease a 9x9 inch baking pan.
2. **Melt Butter:** In a saucepan, melt butter. Remove from heat and stir in sugar, eggs, and vanilla.
3. **Add Dry Ingredients:** Mix in cocoa, flour, salt, and baking powder until well combined.
4. **Bake:** Pour batter into the prepared pan and bake for 20-25 minutes. Let cool before cutting into squares.

Apple Crisp

Ingredients:

- 4 cups sliced apples (Granny Smith or your choice)
- 1 cup brown sugar
- 1/2 cup all-purpose flour
- 1/2 cup oats
- 1 tsp cinnamon
- 1/4 cup butter, softened

Instructions:

1. **Preheat Oven:** Preheat oven to 350°F (175°C). Grease a baking dish.
2. **Prepare Apples:** Spread sliced apples in the bottom of the dish.
3. **Make Topping:** In a bowl, mix brown sugar, flour, oats, cinnamon, and butter until crumbly.
4. **Bake:** Sprinkle topping over apples and bake for 30-35 minutes until golden.

Fruit Salad

Ingredients:

- 2 cups strawberries, sliced
- 2 cups pineapple, diced
- 2 cups blueberries
- 2 cups grapes, halved
- 1 banana, sliced
- Juice of 1 lemon
- 1 tbsp honey (optional)

Instructions:

1. **Combine Fruit:** In a large bowl, combine all the fruits.
2. **Dress Salad:** Drizzle with lemon juice and honey if using; toss gently to combine.
3. **Serve:** Chill before serving if desired.

Cinnamon Rolls

Ingredients:

- 2 cups all-purpose flour
- 1/2 cup milk, warmed
- 1/4 cup sugar
- 1/4 cup butter, softened
- 1 egg
- 1 tbsp baking powder
- 1/2 tsp salt
- 1/2 cup brown sugar
- 1 tbsp cinnamon
- 1/4 cup butter, melted (for filling)

Instructions:

1. **Preheat Oven:** Preheat oven to 375°F (190°C).
2. **Make Dough:** In a bowl, mix flour, sugar, baking powder, and salt. Stir in milk, softened butter, and egg to form a dough.
3. **Roll and Fill:** Roll out dough into a rectangle. Spread melted butter over it, sprinkle with brown sugar and cinnamon, then roll up tightly.
4. **Cut and Bake:** Cut into slices and place in a greased baking dish. Bake for 20-25 minutes until golden.

Rice Pudding

Ingredients:

- 1 cup cooked rice
- 2 cups milk
- 1/2 cup sugar
- 1/4 cup raisins
- 1 tsp vanilla extract
- 1/2 tsp cinnamon
- 2 eggs, beaten

Instructions:

1. **Combine Ingredients:** In a saucepan, combine cooked rice, milk, sugar, raisins, and cinnamon. Bring to a gentle simmer.
2. **Add Eggs:** Gradually stir in beaten eggs, cooking until thickened (about 10 minutes).
3. **Serve:** Remove from heat, stir in vanilla, and serve warm or chilled.

Lemon Bars

Ingredients:

- 1 cup all-purpose flour
- 1/2 cup powdered sugar
- 1/2 cup butter, softened
- 2 large eggs
- 1 cup granulated sugar
- 1/4 cup lemon juice
- 1/2 tsp baking powder
- Powdered sugar for dusting

Instructions:

1. **Preheat Oven:** Preheat oven to 350°F (175°C). Grease an 8x8 inch baking pan.
2. **Make Crust:** In a bowl, mix flour and powdered sugar. Cut in butter until crumbly. Press into the bottom of the pan.
3. **Bake Crust:** Bake for 15-20 minutes until lightly golden.
4. **Make Filling:** In another bowl, whisk together eggs, granulated sugar, lemon juice, and baking powder. Pour over baked crust.
5. **Bake Again:** Bake for an additional 20-25 minutes. Let cool and dust with powdered sugar before slicing.

Enjoy these delightful desserts and treats!